SHAMELESS
WOMAN

D0813835

Other works by Magdalena Gómez

CD: AmaXonica: Howls from the Left Side of My Body
Spoken Word/Poetry
Co-produced with Rotary Records

CD: Bemba y Chichón, Spoken Word/Poetry and Songs
Co-produced with Abraham Gomez-Delgado

Window Shopping in America
Poems for Performance
Limited edition chapbook

For more information,
visit www.magdalenagomez.com

SHAMELESS WOMAN

by

Magdalena Gómez

Red Sugarcane Press
New York

Published by Red Sugarcane Press, New York
www.redsugarcanepress.com

Publisher, Editor & Book Layout: Iris Morales
Technical Advisor & eBook Layout: Adrien Bibiloni Morales
Photo & Book Cover Design: Kayla Creamer

ISBN: 978-0-9884750-5-2
Library of Congress Control Number: 2014941084
Also available as e-edition: ISBN: 978-0-9884750-7-6
First Edition
Printed in the United States of America

For Jim

True mother of my birth
who howls with joy
at every first
sight of me.

CONTENTS

FOREWORD

As a young artist and social activist, Magdalena Gómez was influenced by the Nuyorican Literary Movement, a cultural and intellectual force composed of Puerto Rican artists/activists that had its roots in the most neglected and marginalized neighborhoods of New York City, like East Harlem, the Lower East Side and the Bronx in the 1960s and early 1970s. From that beginning, Gómez readily blossomed into a renaissance artist: performer, playwright, teacher, poet, writer, thinker, and social activist. Whichever medium she engages with, the outcome is predictable: her cultural productions charm the eye yet seriously rattle the brain. Seamlessly combining art with activism, Gómez's work has the habit of tilting our complacencies. The newcomer to her work is certain to be ambushed by it, as was my experience the first time my eyes clamped onto one of her riveting performances. But even grizzled veterans of her art are taken aback by the ability of that art to astound and taunt us anew, by shedding light on all the grand topics of life, like power, identity, untruths, sex, honor, the landscape of childhood, and the terrain of adulthood. We would rather have many of those things left in the shadows and not open to the cold, hard light of truth that her work invites us to consider. But that light always pierces through the dim forcing us to sit and take notice. Erecting firewalls between our inner most sensibilities and her art is useless. Her art gets through each and every time and plays havoc with those complacencies. We are better off for it. She achieves this by creating her own personal environment that is expansive enough to put her in touch with her own strength which then rockets her forth unfettered. You can see the aura that envelopes her when she performs. It's like a flame that would set water on fire.

Talk about shedding new light, *Shameless Woman* is a long awaited volume that poetically explores the cultural topography of Gómez's life. We follow her as she tilts the windmills on those insistent themes of sexuality, justice, equality, exploitation, war, tradition, revolution, religion, spiritualism, conflict, love, innocence, history, youth, even death. In her poetry, Gómez is like a meteorological archer who sends down cleansing storms, with flashes of lightning and thunder, that wash away the cover of her life exposing all, while confronting the observer to deal with inconvenient truths. The poems, which allow access into Gómez's world, and which exude economy, intensity and ferocity, uncannily offer keen perceptions about life in all its complexities. As we travel with her through her poetry, we can feel old and more recent sensations come storming back to her. It's a good ride, but a necessarily bumpy one.

Yes, a book of magical poems, tender and intoxicating, that cover the landscape of Gómez's life. Yes, a book of delicious poems which provide a wealth of wisdom in a manner at once enthusiastic and addictive. Yes, a book of searing poems that takes us through the political and cultural whirlwinds of the times Gómez lived through. But the volume is also a gem of memoir with a strong narrative arc. It contains real moments and events. Thus, it is crammed with relationships, first friends, locales, things, experiences, everyday emergencies – stories and moments that automatically translate the everyday into inheritance. It is a complex landscape we shall never see but which we are now privileged to imagine and understand very clearly.

And what inspired this important volume? Gómez's sense of outrage, a constant hunger for justice and equality, but always with humor, an abiding love of humanity, and an enlightened heart.

Smart, savvy, sexy and sassy, *Shameless Woman,* is an extravagant, inventive, rare, high-spirited, and emotionally sweeping volume that explores the life of Gómez and the myriad pathways that led to her varied cultural productions and social activism. What we owe Magdalena Gómez is beyond evaluation.

More of something is not necessarily a good thing. But the more we can get of the riches of Gómez's creative imagination is a good thing, as this book of poetry confirms. Thanks to her generosity, Gómez has recently given her personal collection, with its myriad treasures, to the University of Connecticut's Archive and Special Collections in the Thomas J. Dodd Research Center. As a result anyone can now spend a quiet afternoon reading through the Collection, an activity sure to take you into the extraordinary world of a great artist.

Roger N. Buckley
Professor of History, University of Connecticut
November 8, 2013

SHAMELESS WOMAN

When I was a kid my mother warned me that once I hit puberty my vagina would look like Fidel Castro; not a word about post-menopausal Eisenhower. I've had to deal with that on my own.

I am known by friends, fans and detractors alike as a *sin vergüenza*. A shameless woman. My favorite words are *toto, chocha, crika, ticket* and *puñieta*. I love consonants; vowels not so much. I am particularly enamored of the letter K of which my first language, Spanish, is for the most part, deprived. However, I take it back when the mood strikes. I have often been told by misogynist men and prissy women that I am "too much." I ask them: "Perhaps you are simply not enough?"

I will have to come back from the dead. I am curious to see who will pretend to have liked me.

A Celebration of Knowing

for Eilish Thompson

If I am called a cow
I say
Yes! Yes!
I am a cow!

Slow, steady beast
eyes upon you
let you know
I have seen more
than I need to tell;
let my steady silence
bring shame to your lies.

Yes! Yes! I am a cow!
My flesh, my bones of use
in this world
my breasts
neighbors to the heart
where the rhythmic dance
of all that is
begins;

I am a cow
bringing forth the substance of life;
I am where your hunger begins
and where it ends.

If I am called a witch I say
Yes!
Yes!
I am a witch conjuring love
where there is fear
healing where there is grief
clear movement
where waters have settled into mud.

My incantation
unspoken word of action

my witches' hands
unfold to embrace,
fold to protect
those in my care;
my belly
a cauldron of response.
My magic pours out as presence.

If I am called a hen
I say
Yes!
Yes!
I am a hen!
I peck at the door of justice
until you let me in!
I peck at the door of justice
until you let me in!
I peck at the door of justice
until you let me in!

Daughters and sisters
walking beside me,
the ancient ones
furrowed in my marrow,
a legion of unhatched eggs;
we have *huevos*, baby,
you know nothing about.

If I am called a bitch
I say
Yes!
Yes!
I am a bitch
of a thousand tongues
pointing towards the moon
howling the prophecy
of uproarious tides
monsoons
tornadoes
tsunami

volcanoes
howling witness of destruction
for a world deafened
by the same fingers
that count money.

Yes! Yes!
I am a snarling bitch.
You squirm as I read your face;
my howl unleashing
night into day
day into night
my mouth full of razors
I tear the veil
between the living
and the dead;
eyes meet
and all are seen.

If I am called a cat
I say, Yes! Yes!
I am a cat, clawing air into blood
when the conversation turns false;
hissing through doors
secrets once hid behind;
the curious, the saviors, the heroes
the neighbors gather to listen and tell;
I kick open the door
scratching your secrets
into headlines all over the world;
Yes! Yes! I am a cat!

If I am called a
slut
puta
priss
hooker
pro
man-eater
pussy

bacalao
tramp
cock-teaser
wench
battle-axe
gamine
vixen
whore
harlot
strumpet
hussy
harridan
old bat
biddy
trollop
tart
cuero
cocotte
demimonde
skank
piece
hootchie girl
chicken head
pigeon
Jezebel
hellcat
ho
doxy
fancy woman
nag
jailbait
fille de joie
cualquiera
concubine
chick
mistress
courtesan
indecente
kept woman

manusiá
paramour
trull
demirep
slit
bimbo
muff
fish
crica
putana
sobrá
harpie
sucía
spinster
cunt

I disemVowel you
with the power of my shamelessness
for I am a shameless woman;
my thoughts and body
beyond your reach.

Your words fall powdered
at my fiercely rooted
I Am Here and I'm Not Going Away
rock steady feet.

If I am called,
named
thought of,
whispered about
attacked,
labeled
any or all of the above
I say:
Yes! Yes!
I am, all of that and more
with *Cunt, Puta* and *Vixen*
my favorite selections
for my own law firm.

I am the law of my own belief
law of compassion
justice
integrity
strength;
I am the Crone
The Hot Tamale
The Hole
through which all come into being;
without me
there is no axis
on which to spin the world
of your thoughts, visions, dreams.

Yes! Yes! I am all of that and more!
I am the Great Mother!
I am the Great Whore!

I am so big you cannot
create enough words
to re-create who I am;
I am all you say I am
and more.

I am all you dare not be;
soft and hard
all at once.
I am all you cannot be;
the one who brings forth gods
without you.

If I am called a Goddess
I say, no my friend,
I am more than that;
I am
a woman
who walks
in peace
because I know
who I am.

Something for the Girls
(grab a drum and read aloud)

These hips clear a path
when I walk
I am tomorrow's body
pay attention child
listen when I talk

my vibe yanks eyes from sockets
down Broadway uptown
with these
Puerto Rican
Dominican
Roma
Arab
Sephardic
hips
love in my eyes
the sword of truth
behind my lips

never too old
to dance,
cut it up
with men
and women
half my age
will not behave
I wear with pride
my ancestral name
I know the place
from where this
vessel came

don't ever feel ashamed
or mortified
by your two full loaves
of sweet brown thigh
a body loved
keeps the soul divine

Beauty is a word
wielded like a blade
selling you lies
in every shade
it cuts you up
then puts you back together
mocks you to the frizz
so you even fear the weather

girl to the mirror
losing the fight
nothing looks good
nothing feels right
kill one more day
sit alone one more night

never just right
never just right
never just right

flick off the lights
before you come in

words your lover
should never hear
never make love
in a state of fear

stop, girl, stop
lay the self-hate down
a queen must never
misplace her crown

dance that body
till you feel it again
treat it with love
like a loyal friend
straddle the drum, sister
as memory's sleuth
these afflictions of fiction
begin in our youth

they can hit us hard
at any time
put lipstick to use
and draw the line
never cross to the side
that swindles your mind
let the blues move your soul
but don't let them move in
you know how a song
can get under your skin

straddle the drum, sister
slap it hard, sister
slap it hard
not to hurt
but to feel
not to break
but to heal
feel the skin of the drum, sister
feel the skin of the drum
hear the ancestors call you
to all that you are

AKIPATI
AKIPATI
hear the voices call
AKIPATI
never alone
your body, your home
wherever you go
AKIPATI
I am here for you
be here for me
this body
has counted
and folded time
birthed the history
and mystery
of a sacred line
a body embraced

keeps the soul divine

AKIPATI
AKIPATI
I will always be
AKIPATI
I am here for you
be here for me

love your body
love your people
love your body
love your people
love your body
love your people
love your body
love your people

every thought
a tool or weapon
liberation or demise
time is short, sister
choose your side

Your ass your own?
or the Master's?
You decide.

Body kept sacred
Keeps the soul divine.

Metaxis*

Taino tongue
in African mouth.
African blood
in Taino heart.
African lips
on white face;
España in a red dress.

Taino ribs
through Spanish sword.
African Gods in Catholic lie.
Salvation at the sharp end
of a soft dialect wet with z's.

In *abuela*'s kitchen
I feel luscious
in my large hips.

At work,
I check my chin for hairs.

A battle cry
soaks in my liver;
outside I smile like church
so you will not call me
a hot blooded Latin.

**Metaxis: The state of belonging completely and
simultaneously to two different, autonomous worlds.
- The Rainbow of Desire, Augusto Boal*

Diosa

Luisa caught the fiebre
passed down from her
tatara tatara tatara güela
brain fever
that kills all the *pobrecito*
excuses for liars
zánganos y *comemierdas*
she will not do *limpiezas*
on sunny days
or cook for *exigentes*
or wear *fajas*
or *brasieles con alambres*
so she is mistaken
by some
as a privileged gringa
by others
as an *engreída*
by some
as an *hija de su madre*
(which she is)
and still by others
as the reincarnation
of Atabex

In bars
at board meetings
in church
in school
      at the market
      in bed
      at the park
      in restaurants
      she writes on napkins:
      "*Know me or p'al carajo*"
      and leaves the imprint
      of her mouth.
      She is a coconut
      making work
      of being tasted.

A River of Recuerdos

(because Juan was not Bobo ni María tampoco)
for Magaly Cardona

I am the woman
you cross the street to avoid.
My lips
my hips
invite you
into a history
dissolved
like sugar
in hot coffee;
it doesn't go away
just gathers at the bottom,
showing up
at the last sip
too much
too late,
but it doesn't
have to be that way
if you stir
it well.

I am *La Fulana*
you see coming for blocks
and cross the street
to avoid;
La Jeba
who makes women
in acrylic pastel
sweater sets
paranoid.

I was the loud cousin
at your 13th birthday
where you got
fifty dollars
a bubble gum corsage
and Kotex.

I told you that bleeding is not
what makes you a woman
it only means
you can get preñá.
I am *La Cualquiera*
who says "preñá"
because I always thought
"embarazada"
meant embarrassed,
and "en cinta"
meant on film.

Anyway,
preñá
sounds more like
what it is
and how it feels
when that baby rips
across the skin border
between glow
and nerve endings.

I was your neighbor
your fellow congregant
at Our Lady of
"AY BENDITO!" church
where rosarios
replaced divorce
as women prayed
for unfaithful husbands
to come home.

I am *La Tía Religiosa*
in the crocheted hat
shimmering in
lentejuelas
the size of nickels;

Presentá
in sleeveless
dresses
who slapped you with
the loose flesh
of her arms
every time she praised Jesus
PRAISE JESUS!!!
You forget
she remembered
every one of your birthdays,
and most years
hers was
the only Valentine you got.

I am *La Marimacha*
La Ésa
of muscular arms
formed in the making
of pasteles;
macha de masa
who drives
all the bochincheras crazy
because they can't figure out
if I'm *La Jota* or not.
Their main concern:
Mosquita Muerta daughters
marrying well
with blood
on the sheets.
I am *La Jíbara*
you accuse
of maligning
the race
the reason
why we are
not appreciated
in upscale
neighborhoods.

I am too Puerto Rican
too loud
don't sit right
and drink beer
out of the can;

I am the one
who calls a hole
in my pants
air conditioning.

I am *La Missy Fu*
in pink plastic chancletas
slapping my way
across winter
sidewalks
my body still warm
from the waters
of Arecibo
and the sands
of Luquillo.

You cross the street
to stay clean
from the dust I kick up
passing 99 cent stores
that try to eat my neighborhood
one penny at a time.

I am *La Agallúa*
in *espandex*
expanded over every inch
of my beautiful culo
that embarrasses you
because it requires
a seat and a half on the subway
where dehydrated women
in pantyhose and pumps
sit with Zabar's bags tucked
neatly between their legs
protected from me

by the Wall Street Journal.
I am both local and express
the papitos in pinstripes
don't know where to get off
when our eyes meet
and my tetas
disobey the cleavage rules
of América;
¡Amén!

I am *La Atrevida*
Sin Vergüenza
Desgracia'
Hija e' Su Madre
who gave your brother
his first kiss
in the bathroom
during Bible Study
at your mother's house
when we were seven;
she has never forgiven me.

I am *La Exajera'*
who can recite the lurid details
of entire novelas
while eating a wheel of guava
con Queso del Pais Indulac
while simultaneously
consulting Walter Mercado
on matters of love
and Lotto.

I am *La Cojonua*
who will never have an ulcer;
I do not hide my anger
or my love:
"¡Estrellate contra el piso!"
"Y que la Vírgen te cuide."
sit side by side
in my lexicon.

19

Yes!
I am *La Loca*
part Mirta Silva
part Iris Chacón
con un chin chin
de Lolita Lebrón;
you cross the street
to interrupt a memory.

I am *La Parejera*
who knows
something
you don't
like how Serbian genius
Nikola Tesla
invented the polyphase
alternating current system;
right now there are people
planning to look it up
because it is really something
that a Puerto Rican
would know something like that.

I am the *Porch Monkey*
in cockroach killers
accused of talking so fast
I make it impossible for those
who learned Spanish
in high school
to understand;
if only I could speak Castillian
slowly slip my tongue
through my teeth around z's
or use words like inodoro
instead of *toile*
or autobús
instead of *guagua*.

I am *La Indecente*
showing up like chichos
at parties, weddings and funerals

crawling up your back
with songs of
Hector Lavoe
and seven ways
to prepare bacalao;

Perfuming
the slit in my skirt
with Agua Florida
not for nothing
but just in case.

You silently wish death on me
excusing yourself to go to the bathroom
where you criticize
the escote of my blouse.

You cross the street
to avoid
the part of you
that loves my strength
but fears it just the same;
the part of you left behind
in barrio fire escapes
where we spent our first vacations
in the rice and bean
sofrito fragrance
of *pobre pero sabroso.*

Making muecas
in the shining linoleum
of *pobre pero limpia*
left yourself hanging
on the clotheslines
of overalls and church ruffles
left yourself behind
in the kitchens of
remedios, recetas y *¡qué rico!*
you cross the street
in Nine West
and Prada;

Cacique lingerie
is all that is left of your Taíno self.

You can't look back
you can't
or you might find yourself
back in the boleros
and tambores
of who you truly are
before you crossed
the intersection of
Spanish into English,
black into blonde,
curly into straight,
luscious into linear,
crawling back
into the Spanish of money.

You can't look back
you can't
into the post traumatic
new order
of a deadened body
and controlled speech,
dipped in bleach,
far from the congas
of Orchard Beach;
you can't look back
you can't
you can't look back
you can't
you can't look back
you can't
or you might die
of a heart attack
from the sheer pleasure
of the memory
of how good it feels
to move your ass.

AmaXonica:
Howls from the Left Side of My Body

This woman will not
be still,
or quiet,
or polite.
I laugh only
when I mean it;
and if I laugh too long
for your comfort
too bad.

I despise pink
except
on the tongue,
nipple,
or clitoris.

I do not dress
to please men.
I will not bleach
wax, straighten,
shave, or tame
unruly hair of any kind.
I will speak my mind
without fear of
dirty looks
disapproval
or incarceration;
callused hands
make good
companions
when banging pots
and pans.

I am loud enough
to be heard
in a crowd;
truth was not made
for whispering.

I refuse words
like *prieto, cocolo*
hincha, jabao
and all the other
imperialist words
we call a *"cultural thing"*
I do not think its cute
to threaten children
with *el cuko*
or raise them
on *los cuentos de Juan Bobo*
instead of Agüeybana.
I do not follow
fashions,
dance steps
or slang.
I do not slam
I jam.
I whistle
with two fingers
in my mouth.

Once a mute cobbler
dropped his hammer,
re-shaped his lips
into a crescent moon,
a star,
a gaping sun
and back again,
slowly lathering
sound into being,
my naked body
outside his window
of perfect shoes
in the sizes of all people.

That day I howled
from the left side of my body,
as the right side wept.
And so I received my baptismal name:

"Ama**X**onica"
the only word
he ever said.

Fear of Sex

Antonio Barreto
was a thin lipped
crooked toothed
brown eyed
starched shirt
muscular
trouble maker

my mother warned me
that men with thin lips
cheat on their women
then muttered something
about the French

I ignored Antonio's whistles
pleading and sighs
for a year
then one day
as if inspired by God
kicked him in the nuts

now that my bones ache
and my mother is dead
I wish that at the very least
we had taken a picture together
at Coney Island
on a school day

being a goody-goody
did not
I repeat
did not
pay off

Chocolate Confessions

The summer came too fast,
stayed too long,
like an unwanted man
you keep around
because being alone
makes you feel fatter than you really are.

The kitchen table with its stains
that won't scrub off
gives you something to be annoyed about
when the kids get boring
and guilt digs a fingernail
into your heart.

When you admit to yourself
that maybe being a mother
isn't always fun,
or even nice,
or even necessary;
and dammit! Why doesn't everybody
just go away!

Let me do the dishes when I feel like it.
Let me eat when I feel like it.
Let me smoke a cigarette when I feel like it.
Let me stay in the bathroom
as long as I want.
Just once, I want the decadence of a pedicure.

With too much time to think,
worms sneak out here and there,
slipping into the soup
and conversations with my husband;
it makes us tense,
so I offer him a chocolate.
He smiles.
That's what his mother did
when things got rough.

So now he's fat
and I'm not,
I'm also younger and smarter.
I feel guilty
when he brings home flowers.

It's hell being married to a nice guy.
And the kids do look like angels
When they're sleeping.

FAMILY

When I was a kid we went to the Loews Boulevard Theater at 1032 Southern Boulevard in the Bronx. It was a Spanish-language cinema, originally built as a vaudeville house in 1913. Going to the movies was an all day affair. My family and neighbors all showed up with paper shopping bags filled with cold fried chicken made the night before, potato salad sealed in Tupperware, a variety of Hostess Cupcakes, Saltines, and bricks of yellow government cheese. The kids toted glass jugs of Kool Aid or Hawaiian Punch. The men brought six packs of Pabst Blue Ribbon, Schaffer, or Rhinegold beers; whatever was on sale. The sound of can openers leaving their little triangles were usually timed with silences or kissing scenes. We talked to the screen, shouted warnings, ran commentary, called women *cueros* and men *canallas*, translated for the gringo neighbors brave enough to come with us, and bought our popcorn and Milk Duds from the concession stand.

There was always enough for everybody. Every joke out of Cantinflas's mouth got repeated at least three times-so we got our money's worth. We never worried about missing anything since we'd be there all day with that one movie, especially in summer when we fled sweltering tenements or in the winter, when the boilers of absentee landlords broke down. Mami always brought King Pine or a can of Lysol to spray away *el meao de gato* smell of the old licorice red carpet. It was our Apollo.

Once a year we hopped the upstate bus and went to *Las Villas* in Plattekill, New York for two weeks. It was the Latino Catskills, the *cuchifrito* belt. The Villa Madrid (where my father had been the cook) and the Villa García were the working class resorts. La Villa Nueva was more on the hi-tone side and featured headliners, like the Spaniard crooner Juan Legido, singing about how he wanted a son, but got the disappointment of a girl and ended up loving her anyway because of her rosy cheeks and good looks. Lucky us.

Most of the bus-riding families knew each other and went Villa hopping, checking out the different swimming pools, entertainment (even if it was just a juke box) billiards and rickety riding stables. Poor Villa Madrid just had an old rusty wooden swing set, but made up for it with the most land, apple trees and the best view. Cards, dominoes, badminton, flirting, chasing chickens, brushing down horses, climbing trees, dancing to the 45s, first kisses, showing off at the diving board, making friends and losing them, kept us kids busy.

Those were the good times.

Lines

in the cane fields you drove out serpents
with flames of wild dancing;
in the mountains you outran incest
shred it with fingernails
gouged it with teeth.
Eventually it caught you, Mami
and sold you at the market
next to onions and potatoes
where you pressed roses against your skin
alluring malaria to rescue you.
Mosquitoes ended their stinging
men did not;
they licked the fever
deeper into you
fever that pushed you
out of windows
into rivers
into walls;
fever that tempered
your soft spots into leather,
impenetrable skin that
repelled rain
and all thoughts of love.
Fever in my blood
with every kiss
you pushed away,
offering instead
a little fist
of rice and beans.

You cleaned
all spills and broken things
into the shine of perfection
the mop, the broom
arrows against insults.

You learned to praise
other women's children:
the ones
with straight hair,
perfect teeth;
the ones
no darker than
an August peach.

You made your way
on trains
and always got two seats
one for your shopping bag;
de vez en cuando
you got lost
signs and maps
hurting your eyes.

You hated the smell of cats
and said so to anyone who listened.
You called all politicians liars
with wives who couldn't cook
assured yourself their children
surely must be drug addicts.
Had your hair done on Saturdays,
made pin curls on Monday
to get through the week
did laundry for the families
of the dead,
made sopitas for the sick,
made your own clothes
adding lace to church dresses
for the glory of God;
made Jesus out of dish towels
and rocked him to sleep.

Every night
you jumped off the edge of the world
in search of just one little dream
your mornings
full of nothing,
you slipped into your uniform
of faith,
sipping your coffee
like an heiress
knowing you once
drove serpents from the cane fields.

No man ever raped you deeper
than the English you didn't speak
your eyes collapsing
into dead birds
always in the presence of white folks.

If only we could go back
and I could
tell you the truth
about who they are
about who you are
and give you all the kisses
I saved
por si acaso.

If only we could rub ourselves in roses
simply because
they are beautiful.

Silent Screams from a Torn Cloth Shoe, 1929

Papi was a *bolitero's* boy
during the depression,
brain scrambled with numbers
room for nothing else.
Run boy, run.
Storefront to barber shop,
cut through alleys;
vomit and gasoline
squeeze through
cheap cloth shoes.

Run boy, run
keep your mouth shut
and you'll do aw'right.
Here's half my bologna
with mustard.
You like mustard, right?
Good boy.
Now, run boy, run
don't write nothin' down;
here's a Lucky.

Papi deeply inhales away
the hunger,
the greasy wetness
of torn socks
soaking deep.

Twenty five year-old body
heavy with shame,
collapses on a broken cot
found abandoned next to dog shit
on Delancey Street.

Fingers clamp tight
around a brown paper bag
rattling with the day's coins.

Jaundiced tongues
of peeling paint
catch a scattered
rain of phone numbers,
birthdays
and license plates
on their curling tips.

Broken coil tattoos across his back;
relief comes with the last drag
on a Lucky.

Run boy, run.

Días de Porra

(Diaspora: From the Greek, diasporá, a dispersion.
Any group that has been dispersed outside its
traditional homeland.)

my lengua kissing in Borikua
speaking in English
afraid of dirty looks
mami pulled me
out of school
to translate our way
into housing project paradise
downwind from slumlord
sulfur bouquets
uncollected basura so rotten
even the rats took Tums
shooting gallery hallway hell
tecatos lining the Boulevard
Mami yanked me out of
Honors English
to translate our way
into the Lincoln Hospital
cesspool where you came out
more infected than
you went in
to translate our way
into sweatshops
for a plate of rice and beans
to translate our way
into a savings account
building a future
three dollars a week
to translate ourselves
into laundromat machines
reading the hole
that separates
whites from coloreds
Mister Lui
kept the machines
looking new

Mami respected this
he smiled and said Mami
speaks *bloken engrish*
just rike him

JES, I said
because it was not
made to last

Mr. Lui wheeled me in a wire basket
waving a red t-shirt
cheering me on

Go drown yourself in the *Reservoir!*
Choke on a *costilla* at a *Barbecue!*
Feng Shui your ass outta my way!
Meet you on *Nonotuck* Street in *Naragansett*
for a *mojito!*
Go *schvitz al fresco* in *Los Angeles-*
Si vous plait!

¡Días de Porra!

Mr. Lui's perfect R's
My imperfect Yiddish
Mami shaping R's into J's
The R.S.V.P.
that is my country.

There is no such thing
as English only.
It is broken.
It wasn't meant to last.

Días de Porra II

Sleepy Mexican figurines
beside toothy
Japanese napkin holders
Mammy salt shaker
next to Pappy pepper
a pickaninny spoon
stirs steamed milk into *café negrito*
on Puerto Rican coffee tables
made in Thailand

buxom blonde ashtray
bent at the knees
no one sees
where the men are crushing
their cigarettes

I play the klutz
now and then
so I can breathe

I am the clumsy cousin
my name whispered with pity
too smart to be retarded
so pretty
such a shame

I hide
shove
insert
all of Africa
into my holes
it pushes out
tearing me into
shapes I don't understand
when I feel like
Morocco
but look like
Massachusetts

blood sifting
through congas
soul longing
for guitars
body living for Djembe
sounds growing
gardens from my scars

I grew up in El Bronx
not knowing
the meaning of clave
I grew up near El Yunque
suspicious of tourists
hating flash cameras
once in a while
flirting with un rubio
something sick in me
broken
longing for blue eyes

Borikua in Bensonhurst, circa 1963

Uncle Tony
patriarch
of our Sicilian in-laws
slobbered my cheeks
with Parkinson's kisses
every Bensonhurst Christmas

Brooklyn was *el campo*
to a Hunts Point girl
two-story brick
working appliances
oak trees
clean sidewalks
ten-cent hayrides
without the hay
in a rattle-trap wagon
tugged by Fratellino
the asthmatic horse
with chronic diarrhea
steered by Old Man Banana
whose name was Bonanno
who swore at us
under his garlic breath
for being
vaffanculo bastardi diavoli
(which we were)

he swore at Heaven as he took our dimes
mangiare le mie palle
all I knew was that eating was involved
(*mangiare*, the first word from the "old
country" I ever learned that could be
repeated in church)

Holiday bacchanals
antipasto
gnocchi
lasagna

marinated mysteries
escarole
turkey with all the trimmings
zuppa inglese, sflogliattle, ricotta pie,
cannoli cream competition
among the ants (no aunts in Bensonhurst)
washed down with a Chianti
that tastes like feet
to children who eavesdrop on grownups

Ant Pauline
commandeers
the kitchen of women and girls
her scolding, reckless consonants
burn my ears

An hour past
the last expresso
sandwiches
brought out for the men
on Florentine plates
Sambuca in Murano glass
anisette good for digestion
approval all around
cín-cín, saluté, cent'ann
the widowed neighbor
grumbles about
cheese and heart attacks
football plays shouted room to room
trucks discussed
toaster ovens stacked beneath the tree
Papi plays solitaire
on a TV tray
listening sideways

Ant Marie
swears
between puffs on a Palumbo

cigar of old men
clenched tight between
corn colored teeth

stu cazzo this
putanna that
everybody's *stunata*
except herself
of course

I hid in the bathroom
till the dishes were stacked
blamed the third cannoli
pujando to make it convincing

everybody spoke mostly English
from the time we arrived
to the time we left
even those of us
who didn't know how
until El Día de Los Reyes
the only day
that belonged to
the out-law side
of the family

Damn Fool Thoughts On My Birthday

You whom I called Papito
saved all your love for 7:00 a.m.
whiskey time Mami couldn't see
working man walking his daughter to school
you wrapped my hand around
the parking meter yours squeezed over it
like somehow that would make it stick
gave me THE LOOK
so no pervert could lure me
by the sweet tooth
not even a yellow *Sugar Babies* box
rattling with the song of
Saturday matinee freedom
my only escape
from you and Mami going at it
with *carajo* this and *maricón* that
and the *puta! puta! puta! puta! puta!*
train from mami's childhood
of horny step-brothers and pedophiles
like it was her fault
she cursed the day she told you

cabrón, canalla
canalla, cabrón
¡mal rayo te parta!
¡maldito huevón!

Pollito, chicken
gallina, hen
lápiz, pencil
pluma, pen.

when learning a foreign language
everybody asks about the cussing first
kicking us back into the stone age
of our scary youth
waiting for whiskey to make you nice again, Papi
the cold snakes up past my knee socks

43

I sing the Good and Plenty song
of the Choo-Choo Charlie man
a thousand jingles keep me warm
from a TV that was always on
Mami called it "company"
warned me with the iron in her hand
not to interrupt with *boberías*
especially when Ernie Kovacs
and his monkeys were smoking cigars
while playing the piano

Mami sorted Papi's socks
during the commercials
avoiding Ernie's wife
who sold Dutch Masters cigars
with her legs. *Puta.*

Mami watched novelas
selling hot tempers
loose women
and Latin lovers
like *alcapurrías* under heat lamps.

Yellow needles
jabbed into my eyes
from a sun that hates winter
I prayed for Papi's alcohol to take effect

In my head, television always on

Winston tastes good like a cigarette should

it's not how long you make it,
it's how you make it long

jingle soup, a tropic of chicken
heating my brain
some mornings you took so long, Papi

I thought you had been shot in the head
like Edward G. Robinson
face down in spaghetti
like Jimmy Cagney wrapped in chains
as his mother changed a pillow case
I wanted to check, go inside and pee
held it in, afraid you might strangle me
with my braids if your whiskey didn't take.

My snots turned to icicles

Hey, big spender,
spend a little dime on me.

Taking deliberate steps
you attempted to smile
(drunk or sober it never worked)
You checked for dirt behind my ears,
squeezed and wiped the tip of my nose
like somehow that was love.

Half a century later
I still shiver with jealousy
when a father
holds his little girl's hand
but not like a reprimand
braces her against December
but not like control
whispers of what is to come
if we are good
but not like guilt

his smile assures her
she is indeed good.

We daughters of drunks
can never be good enough.

We daughters of drunks learn to fear sober
more than drunk when there is no work and
the rent is due.

Papi, drowning in the thimble
of a disappointing life.
I wait for your whisky breath
    of nice
your stagger
    of funny
your slurred strand
of dichos y refranes
to start my day
with common sense dictums

I wait for your arm to reach
from the around the corner of an early death.

I close my eyes to hear you whisper that
you're not finished loving me yet.

Chuchin

Chuchin
word that made mami human
exclamation point for pretty
mi nena se ve *chuchin*
my little girl looks *chuchin*
(some words you can't translate
no matter who it upsets)
chuchin
she said it about shoes
dresses
hair-do's
pocketbooks
(especially when they matched the shoes)
chuchin
said it when she made herself a blouse
wore it when Papi was at work
pulled down over the shoulders
Papi wouldn't think it was *chuchin*
Gitanos don't have no *chuchin*
kind of word
especially for women

Mami stopped saying *chuchin*
when she joined up with the Pentecostals
after Papi died
she was justified and sanctified
because her Jesus was crucified
didn't need no more *chuchin* in her life
went from *chuchin* to churchin'
from *jodienda* to hallelujah
she gave me *chuchin* for my clothes
and hallelujah for my soul
not a word for my body
numb with loss.

Hidden Résumé
for Kathryn Neel

I have come from light
forced to enter its absence
at an early age
went deep inside
where secrets tore
at my happiest moments
fear when things go too well
mother jealous of joy
punished laughter
with neck twisting slaps
bitter father
afraid I'd be a whore
like every other woman
(except his mother)
concerned himself
with my posture
and knee exposure
these sentinels of my sex
missed the perfect gentleman
pedophile who spelled his name
in saliva across my back

Since childhood
I've admired whores
their lipstick collections
assertive tits, loud mouths
switchblades
lack of concern over ripped nylons
their PhD's in scumbag radar
and bill-paying enterprise

If my mother had been a whore
by choice not coercion
        hunger
        exile
        only one day of schooling
        dragged by the hair
        from island to island

splayed for soldiers
fathers watching sons
ejaculate
on her horrified face
had their laughter not
raped her soul

I might still have secrets
but they would hurt less

her jewelry box would be
the coffin for a pedophile's dick
        guaranteed
"You like it rough? No problem."
Mami would say,
re-applying her lipstick.

    Lighter fluid inserted via douche bag
    I light the match
    his mother helps us
    dig the grave
    stake his naked father
    (who taught him all he knew)
    face down; sprinkle with corn
    release roosters
    hungry for cockfights

    His mother thanks us
    the pleasure She assures us
    is all Hers, raises Her shovel
    into the eye of a blind God
    who doesn't know Her name
    it never came up
    during beatings or rapes
    by father and son
    a mother's tears would wait
    dragons burst from her eyes
    a hideous satisfaction
    over coffee and pancakes
    when the job is done

at 23 I was raped
by a fine, upstanding law student
who dabbled in medicine and certainty
that no one would take the word
of a $35 dollar a week Puerto Rican *lavaplatos*
over a proper Mississippian
leather briefcase perfect teeth Ivy League
white boy in the Barrio
those drop dead good looks
wrapped in a *yes ma'm* shirt and tie
old ladies swooned
oh, and he cooked Tandoori

Eighteen hours hostage
arsenal of knives, guns
blood lust phlebotomy equipment
neck, arm, back of the knees,
between my toes
centrifuge
beautiful blood
perfect blood
everything about you is beautiful
beautiful girl
take off your jeans
oh, you don't wear panties?
Slut.
No bra?
Libber, huh?

North By Northwest
he speaks along with Cary Grant,
every line.
Makes me watch the credits roll
Checking my face for approval;
smiling became a hateful thing

    took decades to get a real one back

  he bows for applause
  my hands become strangers
  move on their own

he sets up his tripod
the camera rolls.
Tell me how much you like it, honey
the leather miniskirt he made me wear
while holding his calico cat

stroke the pussy nice, now
stroke the pussy,
you're not a lezzie are you?
That skirt belonged to a lezzie
who broke my heart.
Stroke the pussy, sweetheart,
look into the camera
and smile for daddy.

A haunting:
Does he keep the syringe
in his night table drawer?
The 8mm reel of repeated rapes
forcing me to smile into the lens?
Was my shame a present for his daddy
on Father's Day?
Will boys from my college
nudge each other in the darkness
     of porn?
Hey, isn't that...what's her name?
Political Science, right?
The monkey gets slapped hard.

I have admired whores since childhood;
determined all-weather legs on
enraged stilettos
digging into cold nights. Lipstick
frames a story of revenge.

Movie reel stutters in my head

corn scatters over male
bodies naked among roosters
starved for cockfights.

Mr. Mississippi
pockets full of marshmallows
in a gator swamp
weighted down head heavy
with moonshine sucked down
from my Sister Sukie's enema bag

Revenge fantasy
beats a locked ward and Lithium
never killed an insect
that didn't bite me first

Mama, I got my laugh back
no need for guilt in Heaven
Daddy, I got the me that I am back
no need for regret in Purgatory
Devils can't hurt me no more
their eyes are knobs I twist in the night
jewelry box, burial plot
sand, a tuft of grass
no headstone, no flowers
dogs stop and pee
no one visits

Mami
Papi
Pedophiles
Mr. Mississippi

> My hand loosens its grip
> on the handle of hate now.
> I understand.
> God never knew their names either

Bendición

for Doña Elizabeth Arroyo Cruzado

(Bendición or blessing, is requested by youth from their elders upon meeting or departing. This is a timeless tradition of Borikua/Puerto Rican culture and a sign of respect.)

reaching through
the rags of war shattered
memory
I touch
the crown of my people

Bendición

sovereign bodies
temples of peace
before strangers
in rugged boots
hiding tender skin
raped our women
counted our teeth
golden strand
unraveled from
a Caribbean sun
tangled into
silver depths
of blood mixed
with salt and greed
my people
dancing and dying
all at once
a singular word
commutes between
coconuts and stars
vein of light
betrothing the living
and the dead: bendición.

Bendición
in the coffee fields
school houses
curandera gardens
Bendición
en la cocina
cilantro releasing
a Plena of sabores
into the Bomba of sofrito
where bochínche swirls
in our mouths
bathed in cafécito

Bendición
before Parranda
before La Misa
Bendición
before desayuno
before sleep
before turning on
la novela
in tía's sala
before repeating
the details
madrina has missed

Bendición
in every stitch of
crochet that fancies up
the worn arms of furniture
abuelo has been paying off
since the honeymoon
abuela starches the curtains
when you are poor
you take nothing for granted

Bendición
before Quinceañera
before grating viandas
into pasteles our raíces wrapped

like gifts in banana leaves
from abuelas who do not believe
in shortcuts

Bendición
before the coming
of Los Reyes Magos
shoeboxes stuffed with hay
beneath innocent beds
the camels are grateful
a deep ache throbs
in the cleft of their hooves
the Messiah is so far away

Bendición
entre
mosca
y vaso de leche
Bendición
entre Arturo Schomburg
y José Campeche

Bendición
between visits
to Borikén
palm trees
strung between
the call of the rooster
and the kikiriki of the mall
Bendición falls dead
on X-Box ears
welcome to *Porto Rico*

Bendición
entre dichos y refranes
limber y coquito
entre rítmos Afro-Borikua
Bendición
between
howls of revolution
and Spanish serenades
danzas y abanicos
fiestas y areytos

Bendición
entre jarras de guarapo
entre dengue y gripe
entre bohío y los projectos
el super y el cacique

Bendición
entre boliteros
y policias de palito
Bendición entre justicia
y la causa del delito

Bendición
entre Vieques
y Culebra
Bendición
entre pa'lante
y la lucha interminable
Bendición
entre quenepas
y poesías
Bendición
entre caminos
y penas que desvian

Bendición
entre cuerdas del cuatro
cicatrizes del güiro
la piel del tambor
sus cantos y suspiros

Bendición
entre altares y ceniza
velorios y llantos
espantos y espiritistas

Bendición
entre padrino y comaí
entre *me cago en 'na*
y *eso e' lo' que hay*

Bendición
entre Negro y Taíno
entre sangre y hueso
lo sagrado y divino

Bendición
entre bamboo y flamboyan
playa y monte, caña y machete
entre chancletaso de prevención
y tío alcagüete

Bendición
entre El Grito de Lares
y los Macheteros
entre la escopeta
y pólvora tiznando los dedos
La mirada de *La Santita*
y la giñada del *Cuero*
la terquedad del coquí
y el juanete de mi abuelo

Bendición
tejida en pavas
bordada en guayaberas
forjada de hierro y madera
Bendición entre guerreros

Bendición
entre Atabex y Changó
San Lazaro y yerba buena
entre granos de arroz,
Agua Florida y despojos:
¡pa' fuera!

Bendición
entre peseberes y turrón
entre bautismo y entierro
Bendición
papa
Bendición

Bendición entre
capias y amapolas
entre frituras y verduras
entre casabe y camarón
entre la bruja y el cura
Bendición
entre los tabaqueros
entre Lolita y Albizú
entre sueños
de libertad
entre Juan Bobo
y Mambrú
entre décimas
y dominos
entre adobo y pilón
Bendición entre lo fino
y lo que *e'ta cabrón*

Bendición
raspando piragua
calentando la plancha
almidonando téjidos
cociendo muñecas de trapos
contra el olvido

Bendición
entre el fresco del mar
y el maldito calor
lo que no sabe a na'
y lo que tiene sabor

Bendición entre Don y Doña
Bendición
entre tú y usted
Bendición
entre orisha y santo
Bendición entre
amén y aché
Bendición
entre plaza
y pueblo

Bendición
entre perdón
y rencor
Bendición
entre vida y muerte
bendición
Mama
Bendición

Bendición
Bendición
Bendición
Justicia
alza tú voz

Bendición
te persigo
Bendición
te revivo
en las caras
y las almas
de mi pueblo
cada ser
caribeño
y querido

Bendición.
Bendición.
Bendición.

TO THE ESSENCE

The shimmering green of sea grass vibrates at dusk and heals the soul, if you will allow it. That is, if you are fortunate enough to have access to the sea.

While visiting a beach in Maine, I saw a little boy no more than nine, angrily grab and rip out chunks of soil from beneath shimmering sea grass, tossing the moist cakes right next to the sign that read, "Protected Nesting Area. Please Do Not Disturb." His mother balanced her cherry blossom pink Victorian postcard daughter on one smug hip, proudly looking on at her little man's revelry of destruction.

My only consolation is that one day she will look into his unrecognizable eyes and remember the sea grass and sob until there is nothing false left of her.

Madre de Bomba

(because sometimes we must invent our memories)
for Fred Ho

if I had an abuela
she would have fangs
x-ray vision for men
who make false promises
and a special tea
to make them true
to their word
refilling their cup
until she is satisfied

if I had an abuela
she would carve
dragon heads
into her rocking chair
that come alive
when she is angry
sending fire into the places
where she wants it
away from where she doesn't

my abuela would dance naked
at the Hunts Point Market
in front of the cherries
that would spill their juice
at the sight of her;
no one would dare
call the cops or laugh
I assure you
someone would carry
her basket of yautía
up the six flights
to her apartment,
thick skinned roots multiplying
in her boiling pots
of Borikua kitchen generosity

my abuela would keep a machete
by the door
a rosary in the pocket
of her bata
muggers would
drop dead from a look
and just in case
that didn't work
there would always be
a live mousetrap
in the pocket
of her pocketbook

for rapists
bullets in her nostrils
cobras in her ears
a camphorated river
layered in her breath
alum in her tears of rage
to suck dry
even the thought
of raising a hand to her

my abuela
would have
mule legs
kicking open
the smarmy face
of injustice

my abuela
would not be polite
if there is too much salt
in the bacalao
and leave the table
if there is not enough

my abuela
would love Motown
as much as Loíza
swing from the
branches between Borikén y Cuba
tell you about Blackness
as you stretch, iron, bleach
your hair into submission
offering you the cigar
of intelligence
give you another chance
but not too many
fools belong to worms
she would say
and sink her fangs
deep into your heart
until there is room
for light and music
to enter

penetrar
¡Ay! ¡Si! Penetrar

until you are satisfied

Abuela would be the Mother
of all Bomba
history's clean ocean in which
I would happily drown

The Borikua Who Sang Broken Boleros

Don Sinforoso claimed
the Valencía oranges crate
outside of Doña Hilda's botánica
where for $5 you could receive advice
on any subject and a holy card of
San Martín de Porres
the only Black saint we knew about
in the South Bronx. Well maybe
there were others, but nobody
told me.

Don Sinforoso
(who secretly hated his own name)
called the Black saint
Martín de la *Porra* and immediately
begged la Vírgen María to forgive his
blasfemía, crossing himself,
kissing his thumb,
presumably representing
the Body of Christ.

Don Sinforoso started everyday
with four palitos of whatever he
could get at the Crosstown Bar
for the change he collected
the day before
from the women who couldn't resist
his tears when he sang boleros
with a voice that could grate yucca

Don Sinforoso, always the gentleman
in the presence of women and girls
tipped his invisible hat
extended an invisible rose
as the corner of Fox and Tiffany gulped
the last bite of feminine shadow

He swore in a loud voice that he
learned his good manners in Korea
where he had to kill people
who were better than he was
including women and children
he swore on the eyes of his mother
and the virgin vagina of his sister
that it was *los Chinos*
who taught Puerto Ricans, Dominicans
and Cubans how to eat rice

He swore on the kidneys
of his long dead father
that we are all mental defectives
which was why we eat with forks
instead of chopsticks

Don Sinforoso assured us the world
would be a better place
if everyone would confess their sins
and have the cojones to admit
that somewhere deep in their livers
they hate Negros y Chinos and then repent

Repenting he assured us
would be the hard part

The Waiting Room

for Jacobi Hospital, 1974

It's President's Day
the drone of the Coke machine
takes me the nearest
I have ever come
to Kundalini
twitching fluorescent lights
induce a sudden need
to sleep

children
sicker than when they arrived
snuggle beneath secondhand
coats thinking that at the very
least this is better than school
parents secretly pray
the fever is not *dengue*
terror rattles in the echo
of every name called
and disgustedly mispronounced

grief tears the lids
off yesterday's eyes
my father close to naked
stashed on poverty's gurney
in a loveless corridor
three days before
his death
the stingy blanket of my coat
his only shelter

Is the catheter still in?
Apologizing deeply for his
shameful appearance
staring into the gray tunnel
of my eyes trying his best
to avoid the insult
of loving me too late
his final kiss
blown into the antiseptic air
collapsed like a poisoned butterfly
too tired to reach me

Triumphant snickering brings me back
to the droning Coke machine
it appears my name has been
repeatedly called
and gravely mispronounced
to the great amusement
of the children
smothering laughter behind
Better Homes and Gardens
heads down, lips pressed tight
fevers forgotten
the hospital johnny slips open
my ass brings down the house
and for a moment
I feel of use in this world.

The Captive

for Richard Davidson

body tangled in dirty sheets
breathing deep and sour
poems nailed to pale green walls
where shadows mark the hours

a chain of girls
in yellow hats tied beneath the chin
dance across the metal door
where death begs to come in

demons haunting
children taunting
condemned to loss/to shame/to rage
he stays awake just long enough
to fill an empty, lonely page

he begs a kiss
I stain his cheek
he conjures poems in return
he perks an ear towards the jazz
the rusty steam pipe churns

a fractured mind redeems itself
its thousand voices sing
the final song to take him home
horrific, glorious thing.

Eulogy

Norberto Pérez
was the mayor of the projects
he gave advice to neighbors
on Lotto
child-rearing
and how an occasional rum
greatly improves the constitution

Norberto visited Doña Juana daily
asking for *la bendición*
un cafécito
and the wisdom of her 88 years

Doña Juana *era media santera*
and relayed to him
the current activities
of los santos in his life
Yémaya, guardian of his waters
her framed portrait
in white lights
hung over his bed
kept away nightmares
and other intruders

Norberto's white skin
and African hair
kept him out of Miami restaurants
on his arrival from Cuba

He ate sandwiches
con los bones en el parque
and laughed at the insanity
of the world
his children, grandchildren
and neighbors
all agreed he had forearms
like Popeye

Felicidad
his wife of fifty years
still stares at the living room floor
where he had convulsed
she could not reach him
from her wheelchair
her fingers had grown twisted
from factoría rheumatoid
she strained to dial the phone
with her eyes
their eldest daughter
Elizabeth
was due back any moment
with a quart of milk

Norberto stiffened
as the unexpected guest
settled in his body

Norberto did not make
his appointed rounds that day
Doña Juana's cafécito
sat staining his yellow cup

Norberto cannot be kept
out of restaurants anymore

Another Artist Groomed for Jail

a recent arrival
to the English language
Ángel soon found out
how to spell
l-a-z-y
as the teacher wrote it
on the board in a great sweep
of disdain
for his nine year-old nappy head
hanging like a late August sunflower
yawn tears dropping like seeds
down his hungry face
he understood his name
and smiled not knowing
the meaning of this first word
thinking he was being welcomed
to the promised land
where every night
he helped his mother
undo the tangled threads
of factory piece work
while rocking
his little brother
to sleep
wishing him dreams
of the little red house
in their only comic book
hoping he would not feel too sad
about how hard
the bread was
at dinner

next he learned to spell
s-t-u-p-i-d

the children laughed
when he said "thank you"
the only English words he knew
his seat was moved
to the back of the room
he was *Zamora* after all
and that he was an Ángel
did not count
where order is kept
by rows of surnames

from his new seat
the flag covered
the alphabet

he wrote in his book
over and over again
l-a-z-y
s-t-u-p-i-d
l-a-z-y
s-t-u-p-i-d
lazy-lazy-lazy-stupid-lazy

Zamora kept his book
clean and neat
his pencil never far from him
he wiped the eraser on his shirt
to keep from staining
the clean white page

With each new word
he tried to form a story
from the last seat
in the last row
struggling with his sentence

Liberation

I no longer feel
the need
to help those afflicted
with whiteness,
toothy grin liberalism,
late stage besaculismo
or other chronic conditions
feel comfortable
after they insult me
by accident
amazed and impressed
by my lack of an accent
and the *awesomeness*
of my intelligence

THE INVENTION OF WAR

The most abhorrent question I've ever been asked: *Why is a Puerto Rican so interested in the holocaust?*

The most honest question: *I'm hard. You wet?*

If I had the power to do away with war or sex, I would choose war every time.

Which would you choose? You may think *that* is the is the most utterly stupid question you've ever been asked. But look around. The filo skin of prudery drapes the body of Perversion and Greed; two-headed beast that roars: "For God and Country." "Freedom" impersonates some consumerist version of sex connected to violence. Yes, Uncle Sam does *want* you, and will do whatever it takes to get you, especially if you're poor and struggling in high school.

A dehumanized genital fixation devoid of sensuality, married to the neurotic fear of death, are at the root of war. We normalize death through war in the hope that we will cease to fear it. The fear is however, impermeable but transferable. Cowards will seek immortality by any means necessary. Consumption and war are the preferred stupefacients of fools ... or *pendejos*, another one of my favorite words.

Generation Hipster

(This piece is one of several written in response to the alarmingly high number of students I have met who have never heard or know the meaning of the words genocide or holocaust. I have performed for thousands of students in middle and high school assemblies. When I've asked specifically about the Nazi Holocaust, I've too often seen only a few hands go up in recognition-even by those who claim to have read The Diary of Anne Frank.)

I pray for an America
that remembers "whites only"
that remembers Guatemala
that remembers Katrina
who got hurt
who did the hurting
who got the needle
who got pardoned
who rots in the hole
who got hung
who died poor
who lives rich
who is the Master
who is the bitch
who got away
clean from the gavel
who walks the yard
who flies in circles
an America that remembers
complicity:
Trujillo
Pinochet
Papa Doc
Banks, Bush, BP
an America that remembers
Matthew Shepard
Eleanor Bumpers
Oscar Romero
Trayvon Martin
Japanese Internment Camps
People's Park
Carlisle Indian Industrial School
coerced assimilation
of our First 500 Nations

Kitty Genovese
the millions of eyes
that look away
every day
I pray for an America
that cross references
reality without inventing it

I pray for an America
that knows each thread
of invisible rope
inside our bones
that reaches back
to the cradle of our birth

I pray for an America
that asks unpopular questions
that loses sleep over
hunger
sex traffic
drones
human cargo dumping
into sweatshops
the child at both ends
of a gun

An America
outraged
over labor camp
prisons
women birthing
while handcuffed
homelessness
hunger
the dirty needle plunged
into the heart of healthcare

I pray for an America
that stops pretending
"lack" and "exploitation"
are synonyms

I pray for an America
that remembers
Malcolm X that
TROUBLE MAKING NIGGER
JFK that
WOMANIZING   NIGGER   LOVING
MICK
Harvey Milk that
FAGGOT FUDGE PACKER
Dorothy Day that
CATHOLIC COMMIE BITCH

I pray for an America
that remembers
Al Jolson
Mickey Rooney
Jerry Lewis
Amos and Andy an America that
remembers how we laughed
ourselves sick over white male
slant eyes, *ching-chow* gibberish,
Yes Mas'er, Jap-toothed, *no tikee-no washee*
birthin' no baby double over
Jiffy Pop Popcorn bliss
how ugly it all was in the blue glare
pushing us deeper into the sofa coma
from 1939 to right now
Oh, Johnny Depp
how you broke my heart
with a feather
I thought
I really believed
you knew better

I pray for an America
that can still hear
the spinning wheels
of hate on the
cattle cars to Dachau
screeching
Jew
Jew
Jew

A Good Friday Reflection

We have grown comfortable
with the power of holy water
to douse our sins

we have grown comfortable
with confession
as a way out of accountability

we have grown comfortable
at the sight of crucified flesh

above our beds
around our necks
on our walls
in our halls of learning
and healing
clutched in our hands
hung in our temples
nailed to our words
our teaching

we have grown comfortable
with war
crumbling schools
expanding prisons

we have grown comfortable
with death row and drop out rates
the sight of torn flesh
the grinding of iron
against raw nerves
pedophiles hiding
behind ciboria

we have grown comfortable
with censorship and AIDS
thorns pressed down hard
into our imagination
our memory
the body of Christ is starving
distended with hunger and grief
the body of Christ is at war
the body of Christ is addicted
the body of Christ silenced
the body of Christ is forgotten
the body of Christ is in lock-up
the body of Christ is hounded at borders
the body of Christ breathes infected air
the body of Christ drinks polluted water
the body of Christ is left for dead
on a dirty mattress
the body of Christ is kidnapped
the body of Christ is interrogated
the body of Christ is gassed, electrocuted, tortured
the body of Christ
around our necks
above our beds
clutched in our hands
with the fear of death

and on Friday
we abstain from fish.

Roma Psalm

My father's face,
his mother's hands
indigo lamentations
in the smoke-filled air
of hatred's oven
a spray of bullets
scars the silent face
of an august God
unanswered prayers
crushed beneath
tyranny's heel
sift into bitter soil
sprout little brown triangles
on twisted stems
if you listen closely
you can hear them scream
savagely torn
by a westward wind:
remember us

One of Too Many

Head wrapped in the sleeve
of a neighbor's old dress
the coat is twenty years old
     but cashmere
and to the ankles
     warm in fur
        and rubber boots
dragging to the market
for a rotting piece of fruit
     Her fingers have lost
the dime in her pocket

     The hunger of many days
puts courage to steal
     in a tired eye

She is caught by a young man
with a silver star
hanging from his chest
        like Christmas
she is crying

     He sings a song
of knowing better
     when the years tug
at the hem of your dress

     We can forget it this time

Her boots squeak into a room
     with no light
she confesses her shame
     to smiling high school graduates
on the wall.

     And she is still hungry.

Repentance

(For José Enrique Zayas, killed in Vietnam,
September 2, 1971. The flag arrived before the letter;
"friendly fire.")

José
I have not forgotten
the German blue
of your Borikua eyes
mischief hidden behind
childhood's forbidden doors
where you caught
the occasional glimpse
of adult panties
José
I have not forgotten
playing monsters
in the dark corners
of church basements
while your daddy preached
and mami mistook her
complaints for prayer

I have not forgotten
the dreadful sin
of a kiss
between first cousins
when we vowed to never have children
two days before my ninth birthday
dreadful
dreadful
dreadful sin
to have never kissed you again

I have not forgotten
you sneaking love lyrics to me
in the living room
with your hairbrush microphone
grateful my mother did not
hear in English

pretending *Cherish* was just
a stupid white boy song
I offered you a handful
of Cheese Doodles and
taught you the Boston Monkey
you talked about Boy's High
where you learned to read
the knife catalogue
the army offered scholarships
you promised to write

every week for two years
the letters came and went
in code for enemy eyes
my father snooped through
all my drawers in search of drugs
and found our love

José
I have not forgotten
you would live with us
on your return
until that day
when a father's jealousy
sent you back to fleshy swamps
nothing to come home to
one more tour
letters shorter, polite
no more perfumed paper
or locket of hair
Bible verses in place of love poems
boy soldier preacher's son
led a children's choir
then learned to detonate bombs
a land mine
split open our dreams
and love became a pulpy fruit
of blood and flies
your body dragged home
across the empty sky

your name a lost cloud
full of shivers and shards of bone
I was not allowed to say good-bye
your sister a vase of dead flowers
tried to comfort me
closed casket
nothing to see
it was over fast
a dream
it was nothing
really
nothing
you'll soon forget
and life will be good again

Life is good
and I have not
forgotten you, José
for thirty years
in this body
I have carried a memory
of Vietnam
where I lay beside you
a pulpy fruit
of blood and flies
whispering good-bye
into the German blue
of your Borikua eyes

Time to Clean House
for Cindy Sheehan and the Gold Star Families

Desert sands will not be still
in torrents of wind
the dead cannot be hidden
or draped in the splendor
of ceremonial speeches
there are not enough flags
to mop up the blood of Iraq
or sift cancer
from the salt of Vieques

there are not enough hymns
to silence the detonating hearts
of grieving mothers
not enough thanks
from a grateful nation

sorrow
the language
that binds them
rage
the sound
we can all understand
action
the universal prayer
resistance
the Holy hand of God
revolution
a circle in time
and that time has come

justice
has not spoken English
for a very long time

A Lesson from Boys
with Patent Leather Shoes

If I had the longest legs
I could stand on two sides
of the world at once
everyone so busy looking up
even soldiers
would put down
their guns
for a good long look

curiosity can heal the world

Litany of War

for our brothers and sisters of Detroit

The cities
are occupied
gentrified
petrified
genocide
takes many forms
war
illiteracy
poverty
economically depleted
self-esteem defeated
children hating school
with good reason
confusion
haunts the seasons
rain incessant
pleads for mercy
her cries remain
unheeded
nature sounds her warning
as mothers
weep their mourning
birds watch from their wires
as soldiers aim from spires
we've set the world on fire
for paternalistic liars
America gone the way of weeds
choking stems of flowers
one wrinkled shade of green
adorns his ivory towers
generals strut and preen
taking aim on human lives
obeying the obscene
as merging giants thrive

posing for the lens
caging liberty in pens
dragging her through shame
biting freedom in the scruff
defiled in Jesus's name
the poor all look the same
from the vantage point of greed
their lives dragged
through the scum
of word detached from deed
America the beautiful
his amber waves of grain
will not reach the hunger
of infants nursed on pain
the only parent left to them
when fathers go insane
America puts on his boots
and stomps out his terrain
we ignore the howls of history
and twist her into blame
drink the blood of innocents
calling it champagne
watching from our living rooms
as bombs rape foreign skies
numb to the incisions
sliced into our blinded eyes
with ads for cars and beer
we drive toward comfort zones
hide our fear and doubts
ignore our ringing phones
crawling into bottles
screaming
FIRE IN THE HOLE

On This Day of Awakening

*In memory of Mohamed Bouazizi and for the people of
Egypt; you are bread for a starving world.*

For you, with fists in your voice, who without
arms or rope break the aberrant mule.
(All apologies to brother mule who once
carried water to my mother's mouth.)
For you, who plant lush gardens in the putrid
fields of caution, rousing the dead into epiphanies
and face to face contact;
For you who shame the silence
of tyranny's allies those thugs with perfect
teeth and unworn boots
who tug at straining vests from safe distances;
their only rebellion a rumbling, soft stomach.
Threats arrive from the sewers of greed, where secrets
and soldiers huckstered from their youth are buried
beneath lies of bread.

The helicopters,
the trucks,
the guns,
the planes,
the shadows,
the sounds,
the gas,
the smoke,
the looks,
the signals,
the orders.
Check all of the above for stamps of origin.

Cobra rears up straight from broken ground,
dips her tongue deep into the bruise of night,
writing over Cairo the undelivered letter
to be read by the world.
The promise of the last word
makes The People One,
making fools of governments and masters
who command with broken sticks
poking out from their ears.

For you who Stand. Resist. Rebel.
Survivors and Witnesses: Tell.
Cobra, each and all.
From every pore of every body and soul
a million sets of eyes open at once
on the face of holiness;
a sacred prayer erupts around the world
that in every language sings:

"Not enough! No more!"

LESSONS FROM
THE DREAM WORLD

As a child I took the heads off of my dolls in search of their souls. I stuck my nose into the hole of their bodies and breathed deeply, praying to feel their life force and join it with mine so that they might come to life. All I ever felt was the nauseating stink of plastic.

I find it impossible to believe in the arrogance of a *Uni*verse. Especially since I live in the country that thinks it is the epicenter of that universe. Earth is surely the penal colony of the Multiverse. I've waited since early childhood for the extraterrestrials to trust me enough to visit and confirm. I'm certain they know by now that I'm no snitch.

I have not lost faith. I continue to believe that all matter of Nature whether The Unseen and Dream Worlds, the Animate or Inanimate are connected. All definitions are limited and finite as mystery trumps quantum physics. What we believe will always be greater than what we know. It will not always be better, there is simply more of it.

Photograph

Porcupine came to me
in a dream
without quills
roseate
unprotected skin
feeling air
as if for the first time

It is said we are
the beings in our dreams
I confess
the cowardice
of my quills:

stripped down
to the thinnest layer
frantic feet
punish fire
beg it to return
wild monkey of the throat
screeches to the gum line

porcupine pulls out a little pencil
no eraser, bookie style
just the size I loved as a child
after 14 turns on the sharpener

(14 was how many rotations
I usually got away with
before the teacher grit her teeth
to grind my name)

porcupine writes
on a slip of paper
torn from a notebook
the size of a Graham cracker
(spiral: two for a dime
in 1958; I liked them in
Marilyn red)

porcupine's note,
the handwriting mine:
love unlike war
gives us no warning

I wake up to my country
gone the way of weeds
go stand in the river
throw stones
they drown
I weep
my tears
cling to the ripples

porcupine
spreads on her belly
at the foot of a tree
pretending not to see me

I am in the city
an old man has fallen
on the sidewalk
passerby decide
he is a drunk
as insulin shocks his brain
into tomorrow's statistics
baby in a stroller
dials 911

I feel deep into my pockets
for a lingering quill
porcupine eyes me
from her parking meter
perch

I detect
what I suspect is a smile
my insolence to think
that I know
porcupines

a child's voice
trills across the sky
giddy with weeds
breaking through concrete
as the sun repeats:
another chance
another chance
another chance

love unlike war
gives us no warning

I photograph the eyes
of the dead to learn
who I might be

love unlike war
gives us no warning

women bathe in rivers
of the world
infants in their arms

America drifts by
a tin wreck bobbing
jagged, covetous

men sort rice
on ancient roads
America, the speeding truck
mixes grain with gravel
pisses, spits

I strap rage to my body
commit a suicide
that takes decades
porcupine waits
until I can dream her again
  love unlike war
  gives us no warning

a quill or two
plink
onto the sheath of glass
I call my life
I will pick them up
just in case
a need for piercing
should arise

love unlike war
gives us no warning

I photograph
the eyes of the dead
to learn who I might be

Like Perfect Coffee After Imperfect Sleep

Your hands little
lifeboats
catch my grief hammered face
the butterfly of your smile
lands on my nose
forcing my eyes to cross
and find another way
to see, impossible laughter
dressed in sequins and bells
brash, rude, insensitive
struts to the buzzing
of fluorescent lights
my mouth drops open
breath escapes
heart regains rhythm
Sara the medical receptionist
rolls her eyes
I embarrass her with gratitude
you squeeze my hand in victory
I take note there is no
water cooler in sight
tomorrow waits
by a rack of magazines
Oprah smug in her wig
and latest body shape
stares in the direction
of the radiation room
tomorrow sits
legs crossed
high heels
ready
to dance.
If only death shows up
we'll dance anyway.
After all,
she is beautiful
and always ready.

Christmas Eve in a Presbyterian Church Somewhere Unknown

we pulled over
my husband and I
determined to find Christmas
it was my job to enter first
twin speakers mounted
in the vestibule for latecomers
a monotone repeatedly nailed
Christ and the congregation
to the Cross
shepherds and their lambs
wept from the crèche
invisible to the horde
of wishful thinkers thumbing
through hymnals
left to their boredom and doubts
clutching coats
adjusting brassieres
obligations fulfilled
at the final *Amen*
a rush to the parking lot
home to the kitchen
checking gizzards for the thaw
a gynecologist's precision
of rituals and their gravy
boxes ripped open
with nothing inside
not even the hostage finger
of Baby Jesus
for which the lambs
and shepherds wept

nothing, not even snow

Love Letter from a Spiritualist

What I am capable of:
giving you a smile for bread

wetting a finger
deep inside to
write the verse of my name
into your veins

travel to a moment
we never had
your tongue
inside me
whispering goodnight

raze the walls
that separate
the centuries
invade
your conception
so as not to miss
a moment of your being

robed in moon-black
swallow stars
when God is not looking
yours the only light in my heaven
I save myself
for what
has never been

For the Ghost of Federico García Lorca

My body slips inside your eyes
liquid into all your parts
my feet inside of yours
my fingers relearn their shape
inside your hands
my mouth
an ocean of screams
becomes the sweetest hello
as you kiss me
secretly in plain sight
of the one I have promised
to honor
and do
the air is flat and cruel
shattering
the light
in my eyes
that can see
no way out
of loving you.

Prophecy from the Serengeti
(inspired by a dream)

I live twice each day
every dream a lifetime
Serengeti Maasai child
boy with girlish ways
walks towards me
a crowd of sunflowers in one hand
a gourd of milk in the other
we walk the pace of waning moons
find copper lanterns in each other's eyes
peace descends over us
woven of wind and breath
the wildebeest will not die this year
child now mine forever
instructs
you will find the cure for AIDS
within sunflowers and milk
the dream dissolves
a sheer curtain of sugar over hunger
he is gone
I grab a lipstick
off the night table
to write his message on the wall
in fear of forgetting
I tell only two
who live in playgrounds of atoms
they *will look into it*
observe me with pity
that I would believe
in that unprovable world

a key turns
in a rusty lock
I will never fit between the bars
no matter how I starve
knowing that some day
the world will touch the feet of the
little boy with girlish ways on the
Serengeti Plain.

ENDANGERED SPECIES

Cultural memory is the elixir on which we must raise our children to keep them healthy and whole.

If you forget where you came from why should anyone else give a damn?

Remember and Resist.

In Praise of Learning

Borikua mother
Dominican upbringing
Spanish father
Taino beginning
African soul
I am rice and beans
I am platáno
I am mofongo
I am casabe
I am sweet potato pie
I am El Yunque
I am Puerto Plata
I am San Juan
I am Madrid
I am Abidjan
I am Negra in the core of my soul
inner skin a sweet ancestral plum
don't let this face
some call *jincha* fool you
take you
into geographical error
I am Borikua
I am a source of terror
when I show the depth
of who I am
proud
alive
full of promise
I am the promised land
and don't make promises
I can't keep
I am mango
I am melocotón
I'm from New York City
I am from El Rincón

My heart is conga
My bones are clave
My blood is salsa
my way is suave
I kick up salt in Utah
I read books in Ohio
I plant trees in Oregon
I'm a gay Jewish dentist in New York
I'm a Black attorney in New Mexico
a *rubio* chef in Louisiana pulling pork
A *canelita* school girl in Seattle
I read books in two languages
I code switch while performing
brain surgery
on the descendants
of those who see cockroaches
when they hear my name.

We are everywhere.

Hispanic Awareness

All across America del Norte
we celebrate hispanics
los Hispanos
los Spanish people
los Latinos
los ethnic minorities
los other people

I've come to learn
I am less threatening
as a Hispanic
than as a Puerto Rican
more acceptable as Latina
than as Borikua
and often told
as if it is a great compliment and relief
that I "don't look it"
Census economics
inspire, enlighten, awaken
even Stop and Shop is excited
they sell ethnic products
in the ethnic aisle
Jamaican curry
and canned Chow Mein
take harmonious residence
on the shelf above Goya and El Paso
beneath the shitakes
and across from India in a jar

so now my neighbors
ask me how to make Tacos
I tell them I am not Méxicana
I am Borikua

they get confused
and do not invite me to diversity day
at the local school.

Why I Became A Loud Puerto Rican

(and other impolite stories)
for Dorca I. Gómez

In the library I find my people
on dusty bottom shelves,
but I find them;
history disappears like cotton candy
on the tongue if I don't tell my story
someone else will tell it for me.
Borikua, you know your blood jumps and pumps
djembe? Keeps time to the rhythm of chains?
Do you know the blood of Africa runs through our
sugar cane? Do you know the sharp edge of
El Machete like your finger knows the soft edges of
your lover? Do you know you are Indio?
That Borikén means land of the brave and noble
Lord? Borikén, word of Spirit. Puerto Rico/Rich
Port avarice/the second beheading
of San Juan Bautista

Borikua,
do you know why Lolita loaded her gun?
Do you know Don Pedro
defended our right to freedom, to independence
in seven languages from the halls of Harvard
and was silenced in every one?

Did you ever start a conversation in Spanish
then switch to English in an elevator/in a store/
on a bus/on a train/ because you felt a secret
shame/a fear that someone might infer you don't
speak English?
Your story spun into MIRA-MIRA/HOT
BLOODED LATIN/NO PEEKE INGLE/
CUCHI-CUCHI/CUCARACHACHA-CHA/
CARTOON BUFFOON
assault that keeps us drowning between islands.

That used to be me,
lying to myself
in perfect English
denying who I am
in perfect English
trading my tostones
for Twinkies
my pernil
for White Castle
my Bomba y Plena
for Top Ten
in perfect English

My body
my history
my ancestry
my literature
my power
my people
las curanderas
los guarapos
los tabqueros
las fincas
los montes
la religión
la musica del tambor
la escopeta
el machete
EL GRITO DE LARES

My people
I walked away from you
in perfect English.
Denying who I am
in Perfect English.
I left you on the dusty bottom shelf.

But I have found you:
in English
in Spanish
in Spanglish
with palabra indígena
and Nigerian inflection
clave y castañuela
translingual connection
Santa Barbara of the white face
beneath your womanly vestment
a cauterized muscle
of defiant Blackness
throbs against daybreak
orb and lingam
calabash and chalice
chain and crucifix
survive the Middle Passage;
petroglyph carved deep into bone.
I take my people back.
I take my language back.
Back to the bembe
back to the gandinga
back to the choreto
back to the piragua
back to the jicotea
back to the Yaya
back to the burundanga
of all that I am/all that you are/all that we are/
have been/will be forever ¡aché!

I take my Taína/Africana history back
I take my Taína/Africana blood back
I take my literature back
I take my music back
I take my island back
I pray my Orishas
take me back
history bound in blood and leather

I place you on the shelf
that meets the world
between the eyes;
I stack you in my arms
on my back
I make of you a bridge
between islands
and march singing your name
in all my languages.

I AM A LOUD PUERTO RICAN

And I thank you
Estados Unidos
for all of your insults;
they have become
my poems.

La Pompa

Tito
Paco
Cheo
warriors in shorts
skin the color of cinnamon sticks
bare feet dancing on hot pavement
t-shirts hung like flags on the fence

Tito
Paco
Cheo

liberate the neighborhood
with Mr. Mendoza's pliers

la pompa
gushes a river of relief
toddlers pull off diapers
run from the heat
into paradise
confetti of giggles
sparkle in the summer air
the sour faced children
of *la Señora Pentecostal*
watch from across the street
dry from the wind
of their mother's breath
as she prays for the souls
of the little motherless savages

Tito
Paco
Cheo

whisper and laugh
about the girls they will get
who tease them with lollipops
and rolling eyes

Abuela pulls her shopping cart
heavy with Quinceañera catering
redirects the stream with her eyes
Tito
Paco
Cheo
have seen the candles
she burns in teacups
have seen the power of her hand
across fevers
      broken hearts
          and spirits of the dead
Abuela is nobody to mess with

dogs chase their tails in delight
cats look with suspicion
from behind garbage cans
they cannot relax
Pasote drives by in his Cadillac
he owns the streets
but not the people
he rolls up his window
shrinks behind the glass
Tito
Paco
Cheo
laugh and tell him to eat his crack

Don Pedro
emerges from the door
of the social club
where he rules the domino table
and pays for the beers
of those who can't

He left the Island
when he was twenty
to send for his *novia*
so she would live like a queen
she left him for an American tourist

the *bochinche* is
she sells cheap furniture
on layaway
somewhere out in Queens

Tito
Paco
Cheo
hear a siren
they calm *la pompa*
out of respect
the ambulance
does not stop on their street
they laugh at the speed
and guess the drivers
are going to lunch

Mariela's girls play *Chinese* jump rope
in their bathing suits
run to her for sips of orange juice

Negrito pulls his hands
the size of tobacco leaves
from the pockets of his linen slacks
holds a knife and picks up the Cross
he is carving for *Abuela*
in thanks for saving his little Rosita
from *la melancolía*
that drained her body of light

Doña Ramona
sits on the stoop
and smokes a cigar
the kind her Juan enjoyed
before the police
mistook him for a burglar
in his own home
the sandwich he was eating
wasn't loaded

Tito
Paco
Cheo
hear Mr. Softee
from three blocks away
the tinny tune sends mothers
running to their windows
throwing down quarters
wrapped in handkerchiefs
into little hands that open
like flowers in the rain

La Pompa is forgotten

Tito
Paco
Cheo
are followed to the truck
by a swarm of dancing braids
and smiles
nobody cuts the line
rainbow sprinkles for everybody

Mr. Mendoza
finds his pliers
resting on the curb
goes to *la pompa*
and looks up to be sure
that the sun is indeed going down

the cry of liberation
turns to a quiet whisper
the children are busy with sweetness

Tito
Paco
Cheo
offer licks to the children
whose mothers are at work
whose fathers returned to the fields
there is enough for everyone

Mr. Mendoza looks for Don Pedro
invites him for *un palito*
resting his pliers on the table
where he shuffles the dominoes

Tito
Paco
Cheo

their t-shirts
flags on the fence
wave in the breeze
of simple joys

Para Mis Hermanos Encarcelados

(for the men of ¡Despierta Boricua!
at Ludlow Correctional)

jíbara, soy jíbara
la sangre me lo dice

mami, nació en El Fanguito
pobreza sin nombre
desespero, su techo
hambre, su maca
el agua contaminada
sus tripitas hinchadas
buscaba pan entre las nubes
y no encontraba nada

le dieron mil leñazos
por el colmo de nacer
¡atrevida, desgraciada!
¡otra maldita mujer!

a trabajar como burro
hasta más no poder
lava, que limpia, cocina
recoje lo poco que hay
la escoba, su mano derecha
la izquierda, para el com'pai

alma deslumbrada
vida sin auxilio
sus ojitos apagados
parecían tornillitos

su mente quebrada
sin saber maravillar
las mariposas no pasaban
por ese arrabal

pero un día
algo se le metió
como fuego por dentro
que algunos llaman viento
otros llaman Dios
tormenta en las entrañas
que cobardes evitan
y bravos reniegan
los soberbios lo ignoran
o le tiran piedras

ven fuego ven
te estaba esperando
por poco no te vi
casi ciega de llantos

ven, ven
suelta lo que quede
de mi verdadero ser
mi corazón mitad hombre
mi corazón mitad mujer
todo lo que soy
hoy lo quiero ser

ven fuego ven
ven fuego ven

de ese infierno
con pura gana
esa niña se soltó
con cáscara de coco
las cadenas reventó
un/dos/tres
cién veces lo intentó
esos números son de goma
y regresan vez tras vez
10 años, el uno
10 años, el dos
10 años, el trés
y luego al revéz

gritando su nombre
salió arañando
la cara de la sombra
que la estaba desviando
para que nunca se olviden
las escobas, ni com'pai's
que lo que se hace de la vida
es lo que hay
un/dos/tres
10 años, el uno
10 años, el dos
10 años, el trés

pa'lante y al revéz
el olvido,
peligroso enemigo
engancha los recuerdos
de tu cinturón
llévalos contigo
como Biblia de tu vida
los malos son maestros
los buenos sanación
¡grita tu nombre, Borikua
tu ser es tu canción!
imperialismo,
tuerto y cojo
pasa por guapote
con cada grito que safamos
le arrancamos el bigote

SOY BORIKUA
SOY BORIKUA
SOY BORIKUA
Un/ dos/ tres
10 años, el uno
10 años, el dos
10 años, el trés
y luego al revéz
en la bomba y plena
de Loíza

en las palmas de Luquillo
en las olas del Rincón
desde los callejones de La Perla
lanzo mi canción
hasta el último recuerdo
de donde vino mami
de donde vine yo
vivo pregonando:
libertad, libertad para tu mesa
libertad, libertad para tu mesa
en tu boca miel
tu corazón una fresa

¿quién te negó
el legado al cual nacistes?
solo tu hermano
solo tú

¿de donde vendra tu libertad?
al despertar Borikua
al despertar

libertad, libertad para tu mesa
en tu boca miel
tu corazón una fresa
un/ dos/ tres/ pa'lante y al revéz
10 años, el uno
10 años, el dos
10 años, el trés

¡ven, fuego, ven!
¡ven, fuego, ven!

¡Soy Borikua!
¡Borikua soy!

Invent Th!s!

Primero we had *Survivor*, then we had *The Apprentice*, entonces *Extreme Makeover*, y then *The Inventors*. Well I say, INVENT TH!S:

invent a brassiere that when worn refuses to stay on and tells you why your tetas should be free/ invent a movie that features all people of color that is not about eating, farting, shallow seductions, killing, drug deals, talking to animals, sambo comedy, or any form of tragic event/or just make one less Hollywood extravaganza and feed the people of Iraq

invent a hormone that goes into all drinking water and allows egg and sperm to detect those unfit to be parents and keeps them apart/ let that same hormone make people smarter since everyone seems to blame stupidity on something in the water

invent paper that spontaneously combusts when inhumane legislation is drafted/ a pen that shrivels the genitals of the ones who sign it/ invent a buzzer that goes off every time some incompetent tries to pass the buck or blames the temp

invent a shoe that creates empathy for others without having to walk a mile in them/ invent underwear that does not crawl into the crack of your ass when the weather is hot or you gain a few pounds, invent a pill that eliminates guilt when you eat a donut while simultaneously lowering cholesterol/ invent a pair of pants that not only hug your hips but make you love them

invent a stick remover for the sexually repressed/ invent pocket grease for the stingy/ hobbies for the wealthy that don't involve facilitating training workshops on race and class for the poor on laundry day/ invent menopause for men

invent a condom that doesn't break or fall off
and tastes like Godiva/ invent equal pay for women/
invent amnesty for political prisoners/
invent a facial soap that gives poverty pimps
the face they deserve/ invent a rubber bracelet that when
worn turns battered women and men into ninth degree
black belts/ remember to make them in children's sizes
too

invent a reminder that AIDS is still an epidemic/ that
greed is the biological father of Capital Punishment/ that
Capitalism is the stubbornness of cancer

invent an ejector couch that sends you banging pots and
pans in the streets every time the government tells
another lie/ defiles another country/ invades another
human right/ creates another dog patrolled border/ kills
in your name and gives God all the credit

invent a scotch that gives right wing bigots a hard-on
for economic justice

invent solar power
oh, we already did
invent alternative fuel
oh, we already did
invent organic farming
oh, we already did

invent a plant that can produce food, fiber and energy is
easy and economic to grow, will reduce slave labor and
minimize the exploitation of natural resources; oh, I
forgot, Nature already did.

What was I saying?
invent a left with a sense of humor
invent liberals whose best friends
are not always Puerto Ricans

invent pacifists who are not smug
invent Democrats who can organize
like the Christian Right
invent chads that stick
to crooked Republicans like chicken pox

invent a Green Party without bumper stickers
invent a few more political parties
invent satellites that shoot lasers from outer space
calculating the real numbers of marchers at protests
broadcasting the images on billboards all over the world

invent a pair of shades that makes you see the planet
from the perspective of dolphins choking on flip tops/
invent airwaves that really belong to the people/ or
invent more people who will take them back/ invent a
mop that turns janitors into superheroes who wipe the
ozone layer and corrupt politicians clean/

Invent a sewing machine that gives
the Statue of Liberty a mini skirt
so no one can hide behind her.

Please invent this.

Why I Lost the Popularity Contest

You love my people when we write about cockroaches
crawling through schizophrenic medicine cabinets,
or when one of those little brown soldiers who will
outlive us all camouflages himself in the arroz con
gandules

You love it when we write about the long rusty lines of
public assistance, of white salvation
snorted through our tightly rolled food stamps

You love it when we write about broken furniture
from "jo hab-lo espanol" lay-away

You love it when we write about slave wage
immigrants
who raise your children
and mop your floors

You love it when we write watered down cultural
anecdotes about roasting pigs in the backyard
and betting on cock fights;
you love it when we *were* Puerto Rican

You love it when arrogant academics research from
safe distances hungers they have never known,
excavate social tumors from neighborhoods they
would never live in but visit on safari to insure
continued research funding and laminate veneers

You likee when we talkee funny to make you laugh on
prime time when we tell the stories you expect from
the mind of your telenovela adulterous American
Dream where Lady Libertad turns concubine against
her will in the pleasure den of thieves

You despise our flesh but lust for cheap labor
while fondling our women with your eyes

When I tell you I understand the depth of rage that
might make an adolescent strap on a bomb detonating
into apathetic privilege
when I tell you I understand
despair's muzzled mouth chewing
through the leather of injustice
that revolution is self defense
when I tell you Don Pedro was wired shut
radiated by thugs left to rot
in a hell of cancer and authorized torture
or how Lolita fired shots into the stale air of betrayal
ready to die for her island;

when I sing:

Massacre de Ponce
Jayuya
Utuado
Cerro Maravilla
Alejandria Torres
Dylcia Págan
Alicia Rodriguez
Urayoán
Gilberto Concepción de García
Carmen Valentín
Segundo Ruiz Belvis
Oscar López Rivera
Añasco
Avelino Gonzalez Claudio
Rafael Cancel Miranda
Haydee Beltrán
Iris Morales
y muchos, muchos más
names to be honored
names to be sung
aúnque to den miedo
o te caigan mal

When I sing these names with orgullo for the children

who have not known faces of courage in their lives

What will happen to me then?
When I do not talkee funny?
When I ask what will happen to Assata
when Fidel's too long speeches are replaced by snappy
sound bites of Cuba
the vacation destination
for those in the know with the dough?
What will happen to my voice when I tell you Filiberto
was righteous and the wrong man got shot or that the
wrong people were herded into Gitmo while war
criminals enjoy beers and jokes in their nooks of
leather chairs and unread books;

or when I tell you the Black Panthers the Young Lords
were not the enemy,
but new eyes for a blind nation;
what happens to my voice then?
When I do not write about cockroaches
in the gandules
will not cuchi-cuchi myself into a paycheck,
will not give you what you expect of my people but
take you to the blood bath of Vieques where the
people did not stand down;
take you to the abuelas,
las madres who show up at schools demanding to
know why their children remain illiterate by the age
they are old enough to be recruited for war;
tell you about Eugenio María de Hostos/ Betances/
Lola Rodriguez de Tió/ Los Macheteros/

Tell you that Borikuas died beside their Cuban
brothers and sisters in the jungles of self-
determination tell you that gangs are filled with
mathematicians/ marketing geniuses/ organizers/
orators/ who have had to strap on bombs to feel like
they belong to something that has meaning in a world
that values money and consumption over just about
anything else.

I know
I know
it would be funnier if I wrote about cockroaches in the
underpants of my people
if I did it with an accent
I know
I know
I would have more money in the bank
and you would invite me to more parties
but it's too late
I've pulled the pin; there's no going back and

I'M STILL PUERTO RICAN.

ACKNOWLEDGMENTS

Gracías de todo corazón to Iris Morales and Red Sugarcane Press for this, my first full book in print. You have treated my poems as if they were your own. You have included me in the process every step of the way, regarding my work and my being with great care and respect. I am honored to be one of the inaugural poets of Red Sugarcane, which is creating a new model for publishing that values not only the work, but the personhood of the authors themselves.

Special thanks to fellow Red Sugarcane poet, dear friend and mentor from my youth, José Ángel Figueroa for his support in editing my Spanish language work, along with his colleague Professor José Muñoz, and for his heartfelt and constant encouragement.

Thank you Kayla Creamer, indefatigable, multi-talented arts warrior and collaborator for your boundless patience and generosity and Amherst Media for your passionate support throughout the creation of this book; Jennifer Nieves, hair and make-up artist for cover photograph.

Beloved Bronx, you reared the dragon in me.

Virgilio Gómez, Gitano to the core. For the gifts of truth-telling as a vice, imaginative intelligence as an aphrodisiac, and rebellion as a way of life. Thank you, my father.

Lydia Lajara, Borikua gladiator, for her ferocious survival skills against all odds. She was the worst of all mothers and the best of all teachers.

Jim Lescault, my soul mate, muse, genius, champion and hero.

Lauren Johnson, keeper of all my secrets. Sacred healing sister. Beloved.

Magaly Cardona, holder of my visions and dreams. Sanctuary.

María Luisa Arroyo Poeta Peligrosa of my heart. Sister Warrior.

Michael Surdej, four decades of friendship help keep me shameless.

Fred Ho for fangs to go with my talons. We were Titans.

Daniel Jáquez for welcoming all my langostas y locuras into your life; my theater champion and chosen brother.

George Malave; Rosa Ibarra; Timothy Champoux; for immortalizing me through lens and brush.

Melanie West, you are magic. It was love at first sight.

Trifecta of my 20's: Dennis Douglas, Jeffrey W. Meyer, and Alison Shestakofsky. You kept watch as poems crawled out of my flesh and tended to every wound.

Sara Littlecrow-Russell, you always teach me something new.

Matthew King, I love the Changó you keep hidden.

Kathryn Neel, for the sword with which you protect me.

Naomi Rosenblatt, for the loyalty that still binds us.

Dr. Roger N. Buckley and Angela Rola, my Ellegua and Yemaya.

Marisol Ramos, and Dodd Research Center: history keepers.

Beverly Naidus stubborn in love, life and art.

Theater Gladiators, Rosalba Rolón and Miriam Colón for bringing my writing to life on stage. To all the actors, directors, musicians, technicians and staff who continue to bring my work to a larger world.

Leah Poller, sisters in magic, mysteries and miracles.

Hunts Point Library for Emerson when I was eight.

Lisa Aronson-Fontes, Guardian Angel at the Gate.

NALAC for support, venue and friendship.

Shel Horowitz and D. Dina Friedman, keepers of memory.

In gratitude for my Ferocious Women sisters: Kim Parlengas; Rosemary Tracy Woods; Norma Nunnally; Samalid Hogan; Jean Canosa Albano; Marcia Vilpic; Eilish Thompson; Francheska Morales; Janis Del Valle; María Luisa Arroyo and honorary member, Jeanette Rodriguez, who inspire my life and work.

Abraham Gómez Delgado, Juancho Herrera, Reinaldo Dejesus, Ted Levine, Warren Amerman and Rotary Records for the first recordings of my poetry and songs.

SmART Schools Network, champions of enduring learning.

My friends who died too young. I live each day twice because of you, for you.

Bings Arts Center, Evan Plotkin, Mariclaire Smith, Cafe Palazzo, all of my 1350 Main Street family; the artists, supporters and students who have been on the journey as we carve out venues for the voices of The People during seemingly impossible times. Voices Triumphant!

ABOUT THE AUTHOR

Magdalena Gómez is an award-winning performance poet, playwright and theatre director. She first performed her poetry in a Greenwich Village male burlesque house while she was still in high school. In 2013, her work was received into the University of Connecticut's Archive and Special Collections in the Thomas J. Dodd Research Center.

Shameless Woman is Ms. Gómez's first full collection. Her work has been widely published in U.S. anthologies, magazines, journals and newspapers as well as performed nationally. Seven of the poems in this book are in the staged performance of her work, *Dancing in My Cockroach Killers*, the acclaimed Off-Broadway musical co-produced by Pregones Theater and the Puerto Rican Traveling Theater. For more than a decade, Ms. Gómez was a regular collaborator with the late composer, author and baritone saxophonist, Fred Ho, which included the Caliente! Tour, until Ho's untimely death in 2014. She is the co-founder and artistic director of Teatro V!da, the first Latin@ theater in Springfield, Massachusetts and founder of the Ferocious Women's Group dedicated to creating venue for the voices of women and girls through writing and performance.

Ms. Gómez, a nationally respected teaching artist, was a founding Master Artist with the SmART Schools Network and has worked with them since 1999. Her work is included in high school and college curriculums throughout the U.S. and abroad. Ms. Gómez and poet María Luisa Arroyo co-edited the first multi-cultural, intergenerational and multi-genre book on bullying: *Bullying: Replies, Rebuttals, Confessions and Catharsis;* Skyhorse Publishing.

Ms. Gómez is a commentator with New England Public Radio; a columnist with Point of View newspaper, and a public speaker known for creative keynotes on topics connected to responsible leadership, education, culture and personal liberation.

Ms. Gomez may be reached through her website: www.magdalenagomez.com

ABOUT THE PHOTOGRAPHER

Kayla Creamer is a graduate of the University of Massachusetts at Amherst. Ms. Creamer began her studies as a pre-vet major, but became interested in film and went on to earn a B.A. in Communications. Shortly after graduation, she joined Amherst Media, a public access multimedia center where the public learns to use new and emerging technologies to produce original work. As programming director, she regularly assists in coverage of large-scale projects for local businesses and not-for-profit organizations. *Amherst Media Maker-Faire*, co-sponsored with the University of Massachusetts, was highlighted by the White House.

About the same time that Ms. Creamer joined Amherst Media, she launched *Kayla Creamer Photography and Film* using her film knowledge to pursue a lifelong interest in photography. Her work in video and photography ranges from portraits to weddings and from artist head shots to live performances. She has also assisted in the production of music videos for local area musicians including country artist, Ashley Jordan.

Ms. Creamer is a musician herself and has been playing guitar in rock bands since her high school days. Her latest band, *Next Town Ovah*, is a seven-piece funk band that plays bars and clubs throughout New England.

To find out more about Ms. Creamer's work, visit www.kaylacreamer.com.

ABOUT RED SUGARCANE PRESS

RED SUGARCANE PRESS is an independent press dedicated to presenting emerging and well-known artists and activists from the Caribbean, Latino/a and African diasporas whose works break new ground; broaden our knowledge of history and culture; entertain and inspire. Their thought-provoking perspectives and artistic styles recover forgotten stories and reveal those previously unknown. The work in a variety of genres - poetry, plays, prose, essays, and historical narratives - is rooted in the journey of indigenous and African peoples in the Americas who from enslavement to the present have triumphed through the courage and tenacity of many generations.

RED SUGARCANE PRESS is devoted to the exchange of ideas and collective actions to shape our future and advance movements for a more humane world.

Iris Morales
Founder & Publisher

www.redsugarcanepress.com

Publication Credits

"A Celebration of Knowing," Rotary Records, East Longmeadow, MA, 2004. *AmaXonica: Howls from the Left Side of My Body*, Spoken Word/Poetry CD, Rotary Records, Longmeadow, Massachusetts, 2004.

"Metaxis" (poem in English) with Spanish version translated by Enid Santiago Welch, Peregrine. Vol. XVII, Amherst Writers & Artists Press, Inc., Amherst: 1999. 8, 9.

"A River of Recuerdos" (poem) Upstreet. Number one. Ledgetop Publishing, Richmond, MA: 2005. 165-175. *Window Shopping in America (poems for performance)* a limited edition chapbook, 2007. *AmaXonica: Howls from the Left Side of My Body*, Spoken Word/Poetry CD, Rotary Records, Longmeadow Massachusetts, 2004.

"Chocolate Confessions" (poem) *Puerto Rican Writers At Home In The USA*, edited by Faythe Turner, WA: Open Hand Publishing Inc., 1991. Also published in Literature & Society 1st & 3rd Editions; Prentice-Hall 1994, 2000.

"Lines" Tea Party Magazine, No 16. San Francisco.

"Chuchin" (poem). Luna: A New Journal of Poetry and Translation. Edited by Ray González Volume 1/Issue 1, Spring 1998. 146-148.

"Bendición" (poem) *AmaXonica: Howls from the Left Side of My Body*, Spoken Word/Poetry CD, Rotary Records, Longmeadow Massachusetts, 2004.

"Madre de Bomba" (poem). An African American Point of View Newspaper, Springfield, Massachusetts. April, 2010; *Bemba y Chichón,* Spoken Word/Poetry CD, Rotary Records, Longmeadow Massachusetts, 2008. Co-produced with Abraham Gómez Delgado. Hunter College Center for Puerto Rican Studies. *Letras* online.

"The Borikua Who Sang Broken Boleros" (poem.) Palabra, A Magazine of Chicano and Latino Literary Art. Edited by elena minor. Issue 4, 2008. 24. Breaking Ground/Abriendo Caminos: Anthology of Puerto Rican Women Writers in New York 1980-2012. Edited by Myrna Nieves. Editorial Campana, New York. First Edition, October 2012. 198.

"A Good Friday Reflection" (poem). Upstreet. Number one. Ledgetop Publishing, Richmond, MA: 2005. 165-175.

"One of Too Many" (poem) Ordinary Women, Mujeres Comunes: An Anthology of Poetry by New York City Women. Edited by Sara Miles, Patricia Jones, Sandra María Estéves, and Fay Chiang. With an introduction by Adrienne Rich. New York: 1978. 61-65.

"Time to Clean House" (poem). The Berkshire Review. Volume 14, Summer 2006: 39-40.

"On This Day of Awakening" Poem. The Progressive Magazine, Volume 75, Number 3, March, 2011.

"Like Perfect Coffee After Imperfect Sleep", Tonopah Review, on-line, Volume Two

"Prophecy from the Serengeti" (poem). TweetSpeakPoetry, online journal, April, 2013.

"Hispanic Awareness" (poem) *AmaXonica: Howls from the Left Side of My Body*, Spoken Word/Poetry CD, Rotary Records, Longmeadow Massachusetts, 2004.

"La Pompa" (poem) A Sourcebook for the Community of Religions. Edited by Joel Beversluis. Co-published by The Council for the Parliament of World Religions, Chicago, 1993. 205-206

"Invent Th!s!" "Why I Lost the Popularity Contest" (poems). *Bemba y Chichón,* Spoken Word/Poetry CD, Rotary Records, Longmeadow Massachusetts, 2008. Co-produced with Abraham Gómez-Delgado.

"Why I Lost the Popularity Contest" (poem). Hunter College Center for Puerto Rican Studies, *Letras* online.

CPSIA information can be obtained
at www.ICGtesting.com
Printed in the USA
LVHW042309170123
737341LV00003B/329

9 780988 475052